GEORGE WASHINGTON

Reference Edition Published 1988

Published by Marshall Cavendish Corporation
147 West Merrick Road
Freeport, Long Island
N.Y. 11520

Printed in Italy by New Interlitho, Milan.

All rights reserved. No part of this book may be reproduced or utilized in any form or by any means electronic or mechanical, including photocopying, recording, or by an information storage and retrieval system, without permission from the copyright holders.

© Marshall Cavendish Limited 1988
© Cherrytree Press Ltd 1988

Designed and produced by
AS Publishing

Library of Congress Cataloging-in-Publication Data

George Washington.
    p. cm. — (Children of history; v. 1)
  Includes index.
  Summary: A biography concentrating on the childhood of the Revolutionary War leader and first President of the United States.
  ISBN 0-86307-922-9 (set)
  1. Washington, George, 1732-1799 — Childhood and youth — Juvenile literature. 2. Presidents — United States — Biography — Juvenile literature. [1. Washington, George, 1732-1799 — Childhood and youth. 2. Presidents.] I. Series.
E312.2.G46 1988
973.4′1′0924 — dc19
[B]
[92]

CHILDREN OF HISTORY
GEORGE WASHINGTON

By Brian Williams
Illustrated by Roger Payne

MARSHALL CAVENDISH
NEW YORK, LONDON, TORONTO

A Soldier and Statesman

BRITISH AMERICA
At the time of Washington's birth, Britain ruled 13 colonies that stretched along the eastern shore of the continent. The French and Spanish also ruled large areas of North America. Most of the West was a wilderness, unknown to any white man.

The boy who grew up to be the first President of the United States of America was born on February 11, 1732. His name was George Washington. His birthplace was a small brick farmhouse on a plantation in Westmoreland County, Virginia. At that time, Virginia was one of 13 American colonies ruled by Britain. Most of the colonists were descendants of people who had sailed from Britain to seek a new life in America.

George's family had come from Northamptonshire in England. His great-grandfather, John, sailed to America in 1657. Sulgrave Manor, the Washington home in England, is now a museum devoted to the most famous of John's descendants and most honored of all Americans – George Washington.

"Father of his Country"
George Washington grew up to be a farmer and a businessman. However, destiny called him to serve his people. He led the American colonists to victory in the War of Independence that freed them from British rule. Then he became the first president of the young republic. He helped shape its government, and his strong leadership ensured the nation's growth as a model of democracy and freedom to people all over the world.

WASHINGTON'S BIRTHDAY
Today, Washington's birthday is celebrated on February 22. This is because in 1752 the calendar was altered. People in Britain and the American colonies "lost" 11 days. Washington himself always celebrated his birthday on February 11.

The Washington Family
George's father, Augustine Washington, was a hard-working planter who also owned an ironworks. He was well-to-do, and a member of the House of Burgesses, Virginia's local government assembly. He lived on land he had inherited at Pope's Creek, not far from the Potomac River.

In 1729, while he was away on a business trip to England, Augustine's first wife, Jane Butler, died. He was left with three children to bring up and in 1731 he married again. His new wife was Mary Ball, an orphan aged 23 (15 years younger than Augustine). In 1732 their first son, George, was born. By the time George was 3, he had a sister, Betty (1½), and a baby brother, Samuel.

Augustine Washington, his wife Mary, and young George in front of the house where the future President was born. After George, Mary Washington had five more children: Elizabeth (Betty), Samuel, John Augustine, Charles, and Mildred (who died while still a baby).

George enjoyed watching the land being cleared for the new plantation at Little Hunting Creek. On the site of the old house on the hill would one day be built Mount Vernon, where George would live and die.

A New Home

George's two half-brothers Lawrence and Augustine Jr were away at school in England when sadly in 1735 their sister Jane died. In that same year the family moved house.

Like other Virginian planters, George's father was anxious to increase his estates. Marriage was one way of doing this: Augustine's wife Mary had 400 acres of land that she had inherited from her father. From his sister Mildred, Augustine had bought a further 2,500 acres at Little Hunting Creek. This land, known as Epsewasson, had never been farmed. The soil was good, but first the forest had to be cleared.

"I DID CUT IT"

A writer named "Parson" Mason Locke Weems, in a book about Washington's life published in the 19th century, told a famous story to show how truthful George was. The story tells how George accidentally chopped down one of his father's cherry trees. His father demanded to know who had done it, and George at once owned up: "I cannot tell a lie, father. I did cut it with my hatchet".

George *did* grow up to be very honest, but there is no proof that the cherry tree story is true.

There was much to be done before the fields could be planted. The fieldworkers, mostly slaves, had to fell trees and uproot the stumps. The heavy trunks were dragged away by oxen.

The house the family lived in had been built in George's grandfather's day. It was a small tumbledown wooden building, not nearly so fine as some of their neighbors' homes. But it had a view over the Potomac River, and there was lots for George and his little sister to do, watching the fieldwork or playing in the woods.

The children were in the care of a black nurse who made sure they came to no harm.

A STONE'S THROW

Another story about young George, intended to show his great strength, tells how he hurled a stone across the wide Rappahannock River while living at Ferry Farm (George's next home). But how wide the river really was in those days we do not know.

Boyhood at Ferry Farm

FOOD AND DRINK
Ferry Farm, like other large plantations, produced most of its own food. Every day the family and servants would eat as much as 46 pounds of flour. The fieldhands ate mostly corn. On a really large plantation, with 250 slaves, the consumption of food each year was vast: 12 tons of pork, 20 whole beef cattle, 170 gallons of brandy, and 5 tons of wheat.

ESSENTIALS OF LIFE
In Virginia, household necessities such as pots and pans were looked after carefully. From a bale of cloth, shipped from Britain, the family would make clothes. A gun, a clock, or a set of surveying instruments were even more valuable because they could not readily be replaced. There were very few stores and many items, such as furniture, the colonists made themselves.

In Virginia, farmers often moved. When the soil in their fields became exhausted, they moved on to plant their crops elsewhere. There was plenty of land, and the richest farmers owned huge tracts of it.

When George was only six, the Washingtons moved again. Augustine wanted to live nearer his ironworks at Accokeek. For their new home, he chose Ferry Farm in King George County. The new house had eight rooms, and the family quickly settled in. Nearby was the small town of Fredericksburg, the first town George had ever seen.

George's mother took him to Fredericksburg to order provisions from the store. The town was really hardly bigger than a village. But to George it must have seemed big, noisy, and crowded. There was no school, but the church sexton gave lessons. And so George began his education. He did most of his lessons at home, helped by his mother.

A Return and a Departure

In 1738, the year the family moved to Ferry Farm, George's older brother Lawrence returned from England. He was 20 years old and to George he must have seemed a fine gentleman. He told George stories about England, about the sea voyage, and about how he would like to be a sailor.

When news came that Britain was at war with Spain, Lawrence was eager to join the Navy. Virginia sent 400 volunteers to fight for King George, and Lawrence was chosen as captain of a company. It was a great honor, and George must have been very proud of his brother.

In August 1740 Lawrence said farewell to the family and set off to join Admiral Edward Vernon's fleet in the West Indies. George was sad to see him go.

FIGHTING FOR THE KING

When Britain went to war with Spain in 1739, the colonies in America had to raise troops to fight for the King. In Virginia, every planter's son wanted to be chosen by the Governor to lead a company. One of Lawrence Washington's friends was so keen to go to the war that he paid the expenses of an entire company of men out of his own pocket. Becoming an officer in the Army or Navy was the ambition of many young colonials.

As George bade farewell to his brother he must have wondered what adventures lay ahead for Lawrence. Like other young Virginians off to the war with Spain, Lawrence hoped for excitement. In fact, he spent his time as a captain of marines on board ship and saw little real fighting.

Under his mother's watchful eye, George worked hard at his books. He was never very good at spelling, but was better than average at mathematics. He was good with a pen, and particularly skilled at drawing maps. His mother sewed the pages of his work into a notebook.

Hard Work

George's father was often away from home on business. This meant that there was a lot for George's mother to do. She ran the home and helped to manage the farm; she ordered all the provisions, supervised the servants, and saw to the children's education. She even found time to make clothes for the slaves, often doing her sewing by candle-light.

After the death of her youngest child, baby Mildred, Mrs. Washington was very sad and came to rely on George. She was determined that he should work hard at his lessons, and he did his best. He struggled to learn how to read and then to write. He enjoyed "ciphering", or arithmetic as we call it today. He liked doing his sums and found counting and measuring easy. Later in life he kept careful business accounts and records of his expenses.

Fun and Games

George did not see a great deal of his father. Once, while Augustine was away on business, fire broke out in one of the farm buildings. Everyone lent a hand to fight the blaze, including the children. They formed a human chain to pass buckets of water from hand to hand. Even so they could not save the building.

But mostly life was uneventful and there was plenty of free time for playing outdoors. George loved riding and swimming and taking command of the rowboat on the creek.

George was as much at home on the water as he was on horseback. The Washington children often played beside the river. They had a small rowboat, and George taught his sister Betty to row. When he was older, he would row across the river to go to school in Fredericksburg.

A Time of Change

George's beloved Lawrence came safely home from the war. George was glad to see him but a little disappointed that he had not fought in any great battles. In truth, Admiral Vernon's campaign against the Spanish had been a failure. But Lawrence had done well, and he was rewarded with an important rank in the Virginia militia (the colony's volunteer army).

In the spring of 1743 George went to visit his cousins in the Choptank district. He was tall for an 11-year-old, and loved country sports, especially riding and hunting. He also enjoyed playing cards and any kind of game. But the fun did not last. George received an urgent message from Ferry Farm. He must ride home at once. His father was ill.

Death and Responsibilities

On April 12, 1743 Augustine died. In his will he left estates amounting to 10,000 acres, with 49 slaves. His eldest sons received the largest inheritances, but George and his mother were well provided for. When George was 21, he would own Ferry Farm as well as three lots of land in Fredericksburg and 10 slaves. He would be a landowner with responsibilities.

Marriage and Society

In June 1743 Lawrence was married. His bride was Anne Fairfax, daughter of Colonel William Fairfax. The Fairfaxes were important people in Virginian society. The colonel's cousin, Lord Thomas Fairfax, was one of the richest men in America. George was plunged into a grand new world full of music and dancing, and polite conversation with gentlemen and their ladies.

GRACIOUS LIVING
The "great houses" or mansions of the Virginia gentry were built in the style of elegant country houses in Britain. Fine furnishings and, for an important occasion, fine costumes were enjoyed by the wealthy. The wedding party at the Fairfax mansion, Belvoir, was just such a grand affair. George became used to mixing with the gentry, although at Ferry Farm he had lived in a far more modest style. That house had five bedrooms, but the hall had also to serve as the dining room.

Lawrence married into one of the leading families of Virginia. Wealthy Virginians like the Fairfaxes enjoyed dressing up for a wedding or a ball. The women wore dresses modeled on the latest English and French fashions. The men wore embroidered coats, silk shirts and stockings, and most wore wigs.

An Open Invitation

After the wedding, Lawrence and George rode round the estate at Little Hunting Creek which Lawrence had inherited. On the site of the old tumbledown house on the hill, Lawrence planned to build a new home. It was to be named Mount Vernon, for Admiral Vernon. Lawrence told George that it could be his home too, for as long as he liked. George enjoyed visiting Mount Vernon and Belvoir, Colonel Fairfax's fine mansion. There he listened to the planters' talk of new settlements and unclaimed lands in the valley of the Ohio River, and of fortunes to be made. He spent as much time as he could with Lawrence, but now more than ever he was needed at Ferry Farm.

The Young Farmer

CLEAN-CUT VIRGINIANS
When George started shaving, he used two of his father's razors. Virginian men were proud of their razors. Some owned as many as a dozen, and treated them as family heirlooms. Most Virginians were clean-shaven; only the trappers and hunters who roamed the forests wore beards.

George now took more interest in the running of the farm. Life on the plantation taught him practical and human skills. He enjoyed working on the land, learning to grow tobacco, wheat, corn, fruit and vegetables, looking after the animals and instructing the slaves. The farm's income came from its crops. But the Washingtons also raised cattle, for beef and milk. In the farm dairy, they made their own butter and cheese.

In his free time George loved to hunt and fish and explore the wilderness that bordered the plantation. Among his

father's things, he had found surveying equipment – a sighting tripod, chains, and rods – and soon he became expert in using them. He was particularly interested in land surveying, running measuring lines across the fields, and mapping every small detail.

He often recalled his father saying that "the axe, the gun and the surveyor's tripod had done most to tame the wilderness". With an axe, a settler cleared the forest ready to plant crops; with a gun he hunted food and defended his land against attack from unfriendly Indians; with the surveyor's tripod, he mapped the unknown land and established his ownership.

Colonel Fairfax kept a neighborly eye on George, especially at harvest time. George ran the firm shrewdly and expected hard work from his men, but he believed in treating slaves kindly. Few Virginians at this time thought that slaves should be free.

TRADE AND TAX
The British government controlled trade between Britain and the American colonies. The colonists depended on trade for such items as linen and tableware, which were shipped from Britain. In return, the colonies sold cargoes of furs, hemp, timber and other goods to Britain. Most of this trade was carried in British ships. Trade taxes too were imposed by the British Parliament.

To a boy raised on a farm, the busy Norfolk harbor suggested a world of adventure. George listened eagerly to one seaman's stories, although afterwards he was not sure how many of them were true!

New Horizons

George had rarely been away from home in all his fourteen years. So he was thrilled when Lawrence invited him to join him in a visit to the port of Norfolk where he had some business to attend to.

George was not disappointed by his first sight of Norfolk. The port was busy with tall-masted ships that had sailed up into Hampton Roads from Chesapeake Bay. From the quay, Virginia's products of wheat, lumber, tar and tobacco were being loaded on to ships bound for Britain. Goods were being unloaded too: sugar and rum from the West Indies, bales of fine cloth and tableware from Britain, tea from China, and wine from Portugal.

A Taste for the Sea

As he wandered along the quayside, George was fascinated by the sights, sounds and smells of the sea. He struck up a conversation with a seaman on the quayside. The man's ship had left London just three weeks before. London was "fearsome big and full of people". It sounded wonderful to George. He was agog with the man's tales of the sea, and ships and faraway places.

Why could he not go abroad? His great-grandfather had sailed across the Atlantic on the *Sea Hawk* nearly a hundred years before. Both his older brothers, like most young gentlemen, had been away to school in England. George had longed to follow in their footsteps, but his father's death had made it impossible. Now George wanted to go to sea.

Lawrence, always ready to support his young brother, agreed that it was a good idea. He would recommend the idea to his step-mother as soon as they reached Ferry Farm. George would make an excellent naval officer.

Doing Mother's Bidding

George's mother was horrified at Lawrence's suggestion. She came from a seafaring family herself, but she was firmly against the idea of her young son going to sea. Since his father's death, he had been a tower of strength. How could she manage without him? She asked her brother's advice and he agreed; George must stay at home. A career on the land, as a surveyor and planter, would be more secure than the life of a naval officer.

There was no point in arguing. Both brothers could see that, and so the matter was quietly laid to rest. George gave up the idea of a naval career. He took the disappointment well. After all, there was much to do at home. And he would still be able to enjoy military life on land, in the local militia.

George Strives to Improve Himself

Always a dutiful son, George settled down to improve his reading and writing. He copied out by hand long passages from books. From one, entitled *Youth's Behavior*, he copied out this motto: "Labor to keep alive in your breast that little speck of cetial (he should have written *celestial*) fire called Conscience".

In his copybook, he carefully wrote out no fewer than 110 "Rules of Civility" to be observed by gentlemen. Among them were: to brush his clothes once a day, to keep good company, and to think before speaking. (George had an explosive temper and was only just learning to control it.) What a gentleman did *not* do, he wrote, included biting his nails, talking with his mouth full, and sneezing or coughing loudly in public. This social grooming stood him in good stead when, from 1748, he spent much of his time at Mount Vernon with Lawrence.

The Young Surveyor

Life at Mount Vernon, with his charming, cultivated sister-in-law, was far more gracious than at home. George had learned polite behavior and took delight in conversation and dancing, as well as in hunting and fishing and other country pursuits. He also enjoyed meeting important people who might be able to influence his career.

George was methodical and thorough in everything he did. He had taught himself the techniques of surveying so well that he had become competent enough to earn a living from his skill. His efforts were now to be rewarded with a chance to further his career and see some more of the world. Of course it was Lawrence's influence that made it possible.

A survey party was to be sent to the remote South Branch of the Potomac River. Its leader was James Genn, an

Mount Vernon, Lawrence's new house, became a second home to George. Eventually, George came to own Mount Vernon, then a fairly modest residence. After his own marriage, George spent much time and money improving Mount Vernon, enlarging it into an impressive mansion.

experienced land surveyor. Colonel Fairfax's eldest son William, aged 23, was to go with him. Lawrence suggested that George should go too. Though only 16, George was sensible and steady, strongly built and, at six feet, taller than most men. Much to everyone's surprise, George's mother agreed to let him go. He was overjoyed.

A Rough Ride

The three surveyors set off in the second week of March 1748. They crossed the crest of the Blue Ridge Mountains, beyond which lay the valley of the Shenandoah River. The land thereabouts was virtually untouched, with only a few isolated farms, linked by rough trails. Sometimes the survey party found shelter for the night in a log cabin; sometimes they had to sleep outdoors. It was not pleasant, wrote George in his diary, to sleep "in a threadbare blanket with double its weight of vermin, such as lice, fleas, etc".

George and his companions carried the tools of their trade with them. The most important was the sighting tripod. It was similar to a modern theodolite and was used to measure the angles between fixed points, such as hills. Tapes and chains stretched betweeen poles were used for measurement. When exploring, a compass was essential, and geometrical instruments like those below were used in drawing up accurate plans.

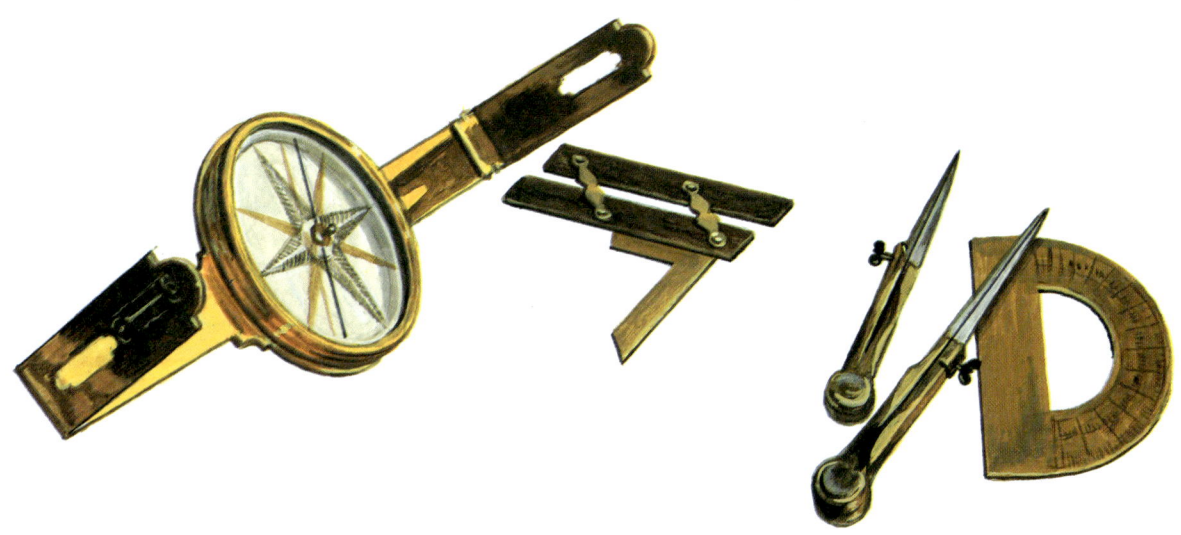

A REAL PIONEER
The pioneer and Indian fighter Daniel Boone was just two years younger than George Washington. While George had come across few Indians, Daniel Boone was growing up in the wilderness, and learning Indian ways. He was even captured, and adopted, by Indians. He explored Kentucky (then a remote county of Virginia) and blazed a trail for settlers through the Cumberland Gap in the Appalachian Mountains. The first town in Kentucky, Boonesborough, was founded by him.

The surveying expedition gave George his first taste of frontier life. He and William Fairfax learned to sleep outdoors, and how to cook game over a camp fire. Although both were gentlemen, they were tough enough to enjoy life in the wilderness, at least most of the time.

Some Remarkable Happenings

More often than not, George recorded in his notes on the journey that "nothing remarkable happened". The weather was wet; heavy rain soaked the travelers and swelled the rivers, making them difficult to cross. George complained that they had had to ride over "the worst road ever trod by man or beast".

It was a relief when on March 22 they reached a trading post run by one Thomas Cresap. The frontiersman's home was surrounded by a stockade to deter hostile Indians – not, he assured his guests, that he had come across a hostile Indian in years. George had hardly seen an Indian in his life. In the face of white settlers the local tribes had moved away westwards. Therefore he was startled and quite nervous when suddenly out of the forest came a band of Indian warriors.

A War Dance by Firelight

Don't worry, said Cresap, these were friendly Indians. He produced bottles of rum, and gave them to the Indian chief. The chief explained that theirs was a war party, but that they had had little luck, taking only one scalp. Then the Indians made a fire, the chief made a long incomprehensible speech, and the braves danced to entertain their hosts. George was entranced by the dance and the accompaniment of drum and rattle. At last there was something exciting to write in his notebook and to tell the family back at Mount Vernon and Ferry Farm.

On another night, the travelers' tent was blown away in a storm. Later they met some German immigrants, whom George described as "ignorant" because they could not speak English. His own companions laughed at him in turn when he failed to shoot a wild turkey at close range.

Success and Sadness

After 33 days in the wilderness, the survey party returned. George had passed his first test, and was accepted as a qualified land surveyor. The following year, 1749, he helped to plan the new town of Alexandria – not far from the place where the great city of Washington was later to be built. In recognition of his skill, he was appointed surveyor of Culpeper County, although only 17.

George earned plenty of money and spent it wisely on land and unwisely gambling at billiards and cards. During this time he continued to live at Mount Vernon. Only one cloud hung over his life.

Lawrence was ill, troubled by a cough. A trip to the local Berkeley Springs did little to help. The doctors feared consumption (what we today call tuberculosis) and advised a warmer climate.

The trip to the West Indies was a memorable experience for George. He was enthralled by the beauty of Barbados, by its lush plant life and brightly colored birds. This was the only occasion on which he left the shores of his native land.

Sickness by the Sea

In 1751 Lawrence agreed to visit the West Indies, and asked George to go with him. The sea voyage made George seasick, but the warmth and beauty of the West Indian islands delighted him. The brothers found lodgings in Bridgetown, Barbados, where their rooms overlooked the harbor, and brightly colored birds chattered in the trees.

Two weeks after they arrived, George was alarmed to find that he too felt unwell. He had a fever which turned out to be smallpox and for three weeks he was desperately ill. Only his vigorous constitution saved his life. His face was pockmarked forever, but the illness gave him lasting immunity, so that afterwards he could travel anywhere in any company without fear of infection.

The Young Soldier

THE FRENCH AND INDIAN WAR
France and Britain had been rivals in North America since 1689. The French and Indian War of 1754-1763 (so called because the French were allied to the Indian tribes) gave Britain victory. Britain's victory opened up new lands for the American colonists to settle. But the Americans grumbled at the higher taxes they had to pay in order to cover the cost of the war.

Sadly the trip did not cure Lawrence. His illness grew worse and he returned home to die, on July 26, 1752. Lawrence left Mount Vernon to his only daughter, but soon afterwards she too died, and under the terms of the will, the estate passed to George.

In 1753 the new landowner's military career began. George had no experience as a soldier but he was given the rank of major in the militia. Conscientious as ever, he read military textbooks to improve his knowledge.

A Dangerous Mission

The Governor of Virginia was anxious about the French who were setting up forts in the Ohio River valley, territory that was claimed by Britain. The French must be warned to stop trespassing.

It was young Major Washington who volunteered to take the message to the French. He rode west with six men. The French commander at Fort Le Boeuf received them politely, but refused to withdraw his men.

George returned home, as speedily as he could in hostile weather conditions, bearing the reply and much useful information about the lie of the land.

On his return from his mission to the French, George almost lost his life. Their Indian guide fired a shot at George and his companion, an experienced scout named Christopher Gist. The bullet missed. Gist would have killed the Indian, but George decided to spare him, and the white men let the Indian go, continuing their journey alone. Later, George narrowly cheated death again, when he fell off a raft into the icy Allegheny River.

Promotion and War

George's leadership earned him praise, and promotion to Lieutenant Colonel. Having enjoyed success, he now tasted defeat. In his next encounter with the French, at Fort Necessity, he was completely overwhelmed and forced to surrender; and this defeat started the nine-year French and Indian War. In a letter George wrote "I have heard the bullets whistle . . ." and was glad he had not been afraid.

George Washington's wife, Martha, was a wealthy woman. Their marriage brought together two large plantations, and made Washington one of the largest landowners in Virginia. The marriage was a happy one, Martha proving a loyal wife and gracious hostess during Washington's years as President. She died in 1802.

Marriage and Revolution

George Washington fought bravely during the French and Indian War. He returned to Virginia a hero, but settled back into peacetime life as a gentleman farmer. In 1759 he married. His wife was Martha Dandridge Custis, a widow with two children, John (Jacky) and Martha (Patsy), of whom George became very fond. The Washingtons had no children of their own, but later adopted Jacky's two children and brought them up.

The peace of Mount Vernon was increasingly disturbed by news of unrest. Throughout the 13 American colonies, people were grumbling – about having to pay higher taxes, about the unjustness of British rule, and most of all about having no control over their own affairs. By the 1770s revolution seemed inevitable.

The Great Soldier

George Washington attended the Continental Congresses held at Philadelphia in 1774 and 1775. The 13 colonies agreed to stand together, and to form an army. They chose Washington to be its commander-in-chief.

In 1775 war broke out, and in July 1776 the colonists declared their independence. Washington molded an untrained volunteer force into a disciplined army. His leadership overcame disasters, such as a retreat across the Delaware River and a freezing winter at Valley Forge, Pennsylvania. Thanks to his generalship, the Americans survived, and a final victory over the British at Yorktown in 1781 secured their freedom.

The American Revolution ended in 1783. The 13 colonies were now states, to be united as one nation.

George Washington took command of the American army at Boston in July 1775. By nature he was a bold commander and a stern disciplinarian, but he had never before led large armies. Though at first opposed to the idea of America breaking away from Britain, he soon came to regard revolution as inevitable and supported the Declaration of Independence.

The Great Statesman

When Washington became President, there were 13 states in the new Union. During his presidency, three more (Vermont, Kentucky, and Tennessee) were added. The new flag of the United States, the Stars and Stripes, is said to have been inspired partly by the Washington family coat of arms, which included stars and stripes. The first national flag of the United States (shown here) had 13 stars and 13 stripes – one for each of the original colonies. Today there are 50 state stars.

Washington felt his job was done; he resigned from the army and returned to his beloved Mount Vernon. But people now asked: who was to lead the United States of America into the hard-won peace?

In 1788 Washington was unanimously elected to be the first President of the United States. He proved a strong leader, never allowing friendship or favoritism to influence him. In 1793 he was re-elected, but on completing this second term in 1796 he retired.

He spent his last years at Mount Vernon. In December 1799 he caught cold while riding about his plantations in rain and snow. Two days later he died, at the age of 67. The American nation mourned the leader who is still admired for being "first in war, first in peace, and first in the heart of his countrymen".

Important Events in George Washington's Life

1732 Born in Westmoreland County, Virginia: February 11.
1738 Lawrence Washington comes home from England.
1743 Death of George's father, Augustine. Marriage of Lawrence.
1748 Surveying expedition to the South Branch of the Potomac.
1749 Appointed Surveyor of Culpeper County.
1751 Visits West Indies with Lawrence.
1752 Lawrence dies, and shortly afterwards George inherits the Mount Vernon estate.
1753 Mission to the French on the Ohio River.
1754 French and Indian War begins.
1758 Election to the Virginia House of Burgesses.
1759 Marries Martha Dandridge Custis.
1774 Opposes British attempt to block trade through Boston. Attends First Continental Congress in Philadelphia.
1775 Second Continental Congress appoints Washington commander-in-chief of all colonial forces.
1776 Declaration of Independence, July 4. Americans forced to retreat across Delaware River.
1777 Americans endure freezing winter at Valley Forge.
1781 British general Cornwallis surrenders to Washington at Yorktown.
1783 War of Independence ends. Washington resigns from the Army and returns home.
1787 Presides over Constitutional Convention.
1789 Inauguration as first President of the United States.
1791 Chooses site of new capital city, to be named Washington.
1796 Refuses to serve third term, and leaves office.
1799 Dies: December 14.

Index

Alexandria 24
Army 9, 29

Ball, Mary 5
Belvoir 12, 13
Billiards 24
Blue Ridge Mountains 21
Boone, Daniel 23
Boston 29
Britain 4, 16, 28, 29
Burgesses, House of 4
Butler, Jane 5

Camping 21-23
Cherry tree story 7
Chesapeake Bay 16
Colonies, British 4, 28
Continental Congress 29
Cresap, Thomas 23
Crops 14, 15
Culpeper County 24
Custis, Martha 28

Declaration of
 Independence 29
Delaware River 29

Education 8, 10, 18
England, visited by
 Lawrence 8
Epsewasson 6

Fairfax, Anne 12
Fairfax, Thomas 12
Fairfax, William 12, 15
Fairfax, William Jr 21
Farming 14, 15
Fashion 12, 13
Ferry Farm 8-15
Fredericksburg 8, 11, 12

French and Indian War 27, 28

Genn, James 20
George III, King 8
Gist, Christopher 27

Indians 23, 27
Inheritance 6, 12, 27

Little Hunting Creek 6, 7

Mathematics 10
Mount Vernon 6, 13, 20, 24, 28, 30

Navy, 8, 9, 16
Norfolk, Virginia 16

Ohio River valley 13, 27

Philadelphia 29
Plantation life 7-11, 14, 15
Pope's Creek 4
Potomac River 4, 7, 20
President 4, 30

Rappahannock River 7
Revolutionary War 29
Riding 11
Rowing 11
Rules of Civility 18

Schoolwork 8, 10, 18
Sea Hawk 17
Shaving 14
Slaves 7, 10, 12, 15
Smallpox 25
Society 12, 13, 18
Spain, war with 8, 9
Stars and Stripes 30
Sulgrave Manor 4
Surveying 15, 20-24
Swimming 11

Taxes 16, 27
Trade 16

Valley Forge 29
Vernon, Edward 8, 12, 13
Virginia 4, 8, 9, 12, 13, 16, 28
Virginia militia 12
Virginia, Governor of 27

Washington, Augustine 4, 5, 8, 12
Washington, Augustine Jr 6
Washington, Betty 5, 11
Washington, city of 24
Washington, George 4-31
 assassination attempt 26, 27; birth 4, 5; birthday 4; death 30; education 8, 10, 18; farming 14, 15; gambling 24; Indian encounter 23; marriage 28; military career 27, 29; navy 16, 18; president 30; smallpox infection 25; social life 12, 13, 18; surveyor 20-24; West Indies visit 25.
Washington, Jane 6
Washington, John 4
Washington, John (Jacky) 28
Washington, Lawrence 6, 8, 9, 12, 13, 16, 18, 24, 25, 27
Washington, Martha (Patsy) 28
Washington, Mary 5, 6, 8, 10, 18, 19, 21
Washington, Mildred 5, 10
Washington, Samuel 5
Weems, Mason Locke
West Indies 16, 25

Yorktown 29
Youth's Behavior 18